Bethea verDorn

Moon Glows

Illustrated by Thomas Graham

Arcade Publishing | New York | LITTLE, BROWN AND COMPANY

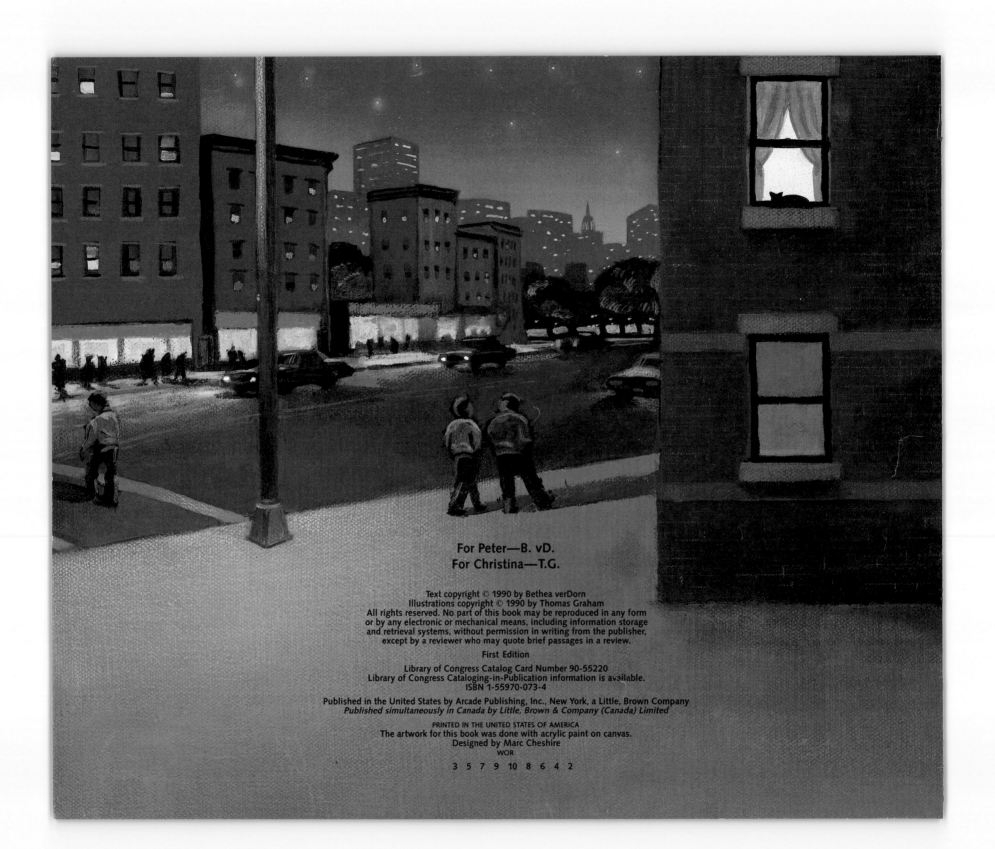

For Peter—B. vD.

For Christina—T.G.

First Edition

Library of Congress Catalog Card Number 90-55220
Library of Congress Cataloging-in-Publication information is available.
ISBN 1-55970-073-4

Published in the United States by Arcade Publishing, Inc., New York, a Little, Brown Company
Published simultaneously in Canada by Little, Brown & Company (Canada) Limited

PRINTED IN THE UNITED STATES OF AMERICA
The artwork for this book was done with acrylic paint on canvas.
Designed by Marc Cheshire
WOR

3 5 7 9 10 8 6 4 2

Moon glows, and city lights sparkle in the city night.
People rush through the night, to and fro in the night;

but sleepy cat curls up at the window.

Moon glows, and harbor lights shimmer in the river night.
Boats tug in the night and sail through the night;

but sleepy fish is silent and still.

Moon glows, and highway lights flash in the highway night.
Cars hum in the night. Trucks speed through the night;

while sleepy turtle tucks himself in his shell.

Moon glows, and barn light gleams in the farmyard night.
Clouds gather in the night. Thunder roars through the night;

but sleepy calf lies cozy and warm.

Moon glows, and cabin lights flicker in the mountain night.
Wind blows in the night. Snow falls through the night;

but sleepy dog stretches out by the fire.

Moon glows, and searchlights blaze in the airport night.
Planes soar in the night. Travelers wait through the night;

while sleepy mouse creeps away to his hole.

Moon glows, and yard lights shine in the backyard night.
Neighbors laugh in the night, call out in the night;

but sleepy sparrow perches high in a tree.

Moon glows, and lamplights glimmer in the bedroom night. Mother sings in the night. Father turns out the light;

while sleepy child dreams with the moon.